Who of Pirates

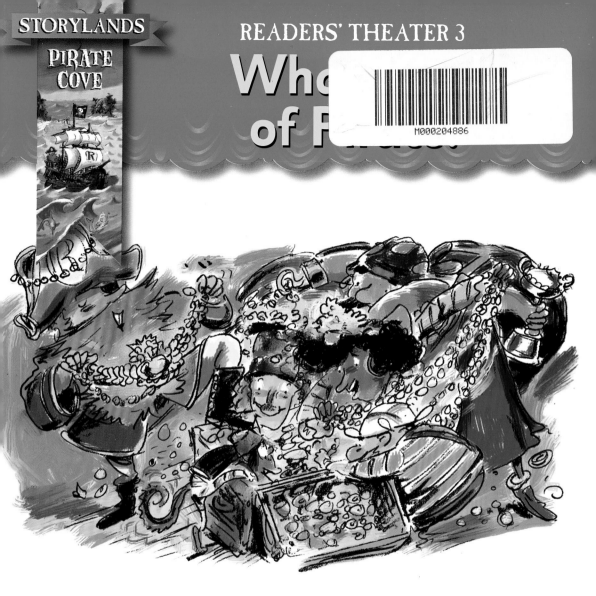

Written by Lisa Thompson
Pictures by Craig Smith

INTRODUCTION

Captain Red Beard and his crew of pirates like meeting other pirates. Then they can steal their treasure! But what happens when they meet the nastiest pirates on the seven seas?

SETTING

Four different pirate ships out at sea — The ship's names are The Black Beast, The Lounge Lizard, The Fooaroo, and The Nasty Rat.

CHARACTERS

Narrator

Captain Red Beard

Fingers the parrot

Crew

Captain Lizard

The lazy crew

Captain Foohoo

The silly crew

Captain Rat

The nasty crew

Narrator: Somewhere on the seven seas is a pirate called Captain Red Beard. The Captain has a ship called The Black Beast. It is a very fine pirate ship. Captain Red Beard and his crew like dropping in on other pirate ships and stealing their treasure.

Fingers: Pirate ship on the starboard bow, Captain.

Captain:
Red Beard Good spotting, Fingers. Happy seadogs! Let's meet them.

Ahoy there fellow pirates! Can my crew and I board your ship? We could swap a few pirate tales of terror and treasure.

Narrator: There was no answer from the ship. Captain Red Beard and his crew boarded it anyway. On board, they saw the ship was a mess and everyone was sleeping.

5

Captain: Shiver me seadogs! What kind of
Red Beard pirates are you? It's the middle of
the day and you're all asleep!

Crew: Look at the state of this ship.

Captain: Keep your voices down. I am
Lizard Captain Lizard and this is my lazy
crew. We were all having a nap
because this is my lazy ship, The
Lounge Lizard. We are the laziest
pirates on the seven seas.

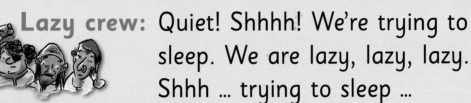

Lazy crew: Quiet! Shhhh! We're trying to sleep. We are lazy, lazy, lazy. Shhh ... trying to sleep ...

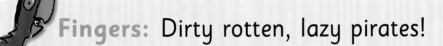

Fingers: Dirty rotten, lazy pirates!

Narrator: Captain Red Beard had an idea.

Captain: Red Beard
Lazy? Yes, I can see that. You are the laziest pirates at sea. Sorry we woke you. We would like to help you go back to sleep. My crew will hum a tune for you.

Crew: (Hum *Twinkle, Twinkle Little Star*.)

Narrator: The humming sent Captain Lizard and his crew into a deep, deep sleep.

8

Captain: Red Beard Now, let's find some treasure.

Crew: We found some gold! We found some silver! We found lots of treasure!

Narrator: The Black Beast set sail over the seven seas in search of more pirates.

Fingers: Pirate ship on the starboard bow, Captain.

9

Captain: Happy seadogs! Let's meet them.
Red Beard Ahoy there fellow pirates! Can my crew and I board your ship? We could swap some tales of terror and treasure.

Narrator: The new ship was covered in red, purple, and yellow dots. The ship was full of laughter and giggles. Once aboard, Captain Red Beard found the giggling captain and her crew. They were dancing and making silly faces.

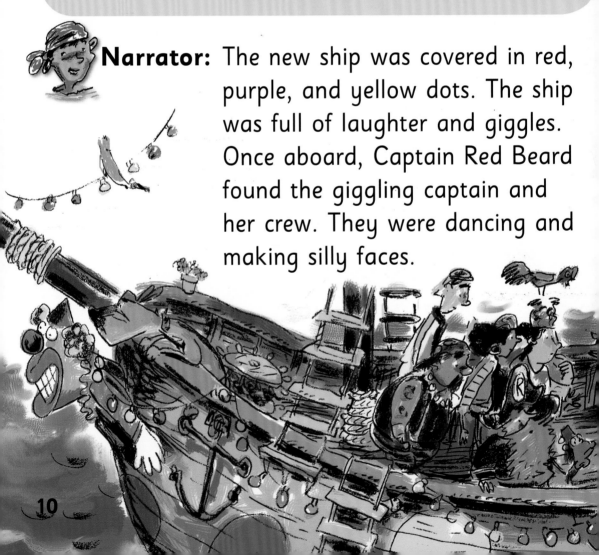

Captain:
Red Beard
Shiver me seadogs! What kind of pirates are you? You are all acting rather silly.

Captain:
Foohoo
Welcome aboard! I am Captain Foohoo and you are on board my ship, The Fooaroo. This is my silly crew.

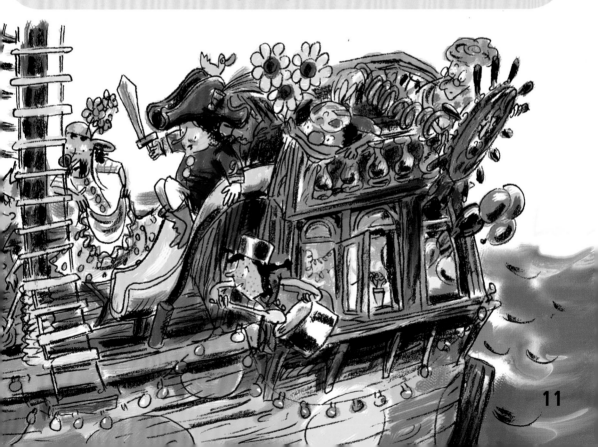

 **Silly crew:** We are the silly, silly, silly crew of The Fooaroo. No crew or captain is sillier than us!

 **Fingers:** Dirty rotten, silly pirates!

 Narrator: Captain Red Beard had an idea.

Captain:
Red Beard Silly? Yes, you are the silliest pirates on the seven seas. We would like to help you to be even sillier. My crew would like to show you a very silly move.

Narrator: All the silly crew of The Fooaroo did the silly move. They rolled their legs over their shoulders. Then, they put their hands behind their knees. It was a very silly move to do because now they were all struck.

13

 **Captain:** Now, let's find some treasure.
Red Beard

 **Crew:** We found some gold! We found some silver! We found lots of treasure!

 Narrator: The Black Beast set sail over the seven seas in search of more pirates.

 Fingers: Pirate ship on the starboard bow, Captain.

Captain: Happy seadogs! Let's meet them.
Red Beard Ahoy there fellow pirates!
Can my crew and I board your
ship? We could swap a few tales
of terror and treasure.

Narrator: Captain Red Beard and his crew
could hear pirates sneering and
swords swishing.

Captain Rat: Aye! Who be YOU pirates who
board my ship?

15

Captain: Red Beard Shiver me seadogs! What kind of pirates are you? Where are your manners?

Captain Rat: Manners? We don't have manners! We are the nastiest pirates on the seven seas.

Nasty crew: We are the nastiest pirates you will ever meet. There are no nastier pirates than us. We are nasty, nasty, nasty.

Fingers: Dirty rotten, nasty pirates!

Narrator: Captain Red Beard had an idea.

Captain Red Beard: Nasty? Yes, you are the nastiest pirates I have ever met. We would like to help you be nasty. You must decide on the nastiest thing you can to do to us. My crew will go below decks while you have a nasty little meeting about it.

Narrator: Captain Rat thought this was a wonderfully nasty idea. His crew all argued about what was nastiest. Captain Red Beard and his crew went below. They filled their pockets with treasure.

Crew: We found some gold! We found some silver! We found lots of treasure!

Captain Rat: Avast, Captain Red Beard and your scurvy crew! We have decided on the nastiest thing. You must all walk the plank!

Captain Red Beard: Oh, Captain Rat, that is nasty!

Crew: Yes Captain Rat, that is a very, very nasty idea!

19

Narrator: Captain Red Beard and his crew walked the plank. Each of them did their best dive into the sea. Some did somersaults. Lizzie even did a triple flip.

Captain Rat: Shiver me sea dogs! What kind of pirates are you? You did not sink! You can all float!

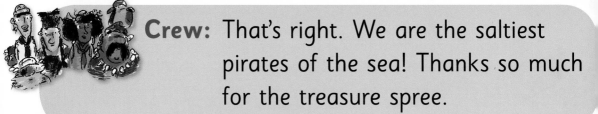

Crew: That's right. We are the saltiest pirates of the sea! Thanks so much for the treasure spree.

Narrator: And with that, The Nasty Rat began to sink. Captain Red Beard had made a nasty hole in the hull.

Captain Red Beard Let's get back to the ship and set sail. We must search for more pirates.

Crew: Aye, aye Captain!

Fingers: We are dirty, rotten, salty pirates!

MAKE SOME SIMPLE PROPS

Four ships are needed — with four name plates: The Black
Beast, The Lounge Lizard, The Fooaroo, and The Nasty Rat.
Fingers needs a telescope.
There must be a plank to walk and gold and silver to
represent treasure.
The crews need some eye patches and bandanas.

You will need:
✓ Cardboard — large sheets
✓ Paints or crayons
✓ Sticky tape, glue
✓ A plank
✓ Red, purple, and yellow paper
✓ Long cardboard tube (or three toilet paper tubes)
✓ Scrap pieces of material
✓ Black cardboard and hat elastic
✓ Gold and silver cardboard and paper

Make the ships

1. Draw the side view of a pirate ship onto cardboard.
   Make it large. Repeat three times.
2. Paint and color the sides to look like pirate ships.
3. Write the four ships' names boldly on the bows.
4. Cut circles from the red, yellow, and purple paper and
   stick them on The Fooaroo.

Make a telescope

1. Use the long cardboard cylinder or join the three smaller ones together.
2. Paint the outside to look like a telescope.

Make eye patches and bandanas for the crews

1. Cut a template students can use to cut eye patches from the black cardboard.
2. Use a hole punch to make holes in either side of the patches.
3. Thread and tie hat elastic through the holes.
4. Cut large triangles from the scrap material — must be large enough to tie around heads as bandanas.

Make treasure

1. Use gold and silver cardboard to cut out treasure coins.
2. Make gold and silver paper chains.
3. Draw and cut out gold/silver goblets and plates.

Which pirate crew would you like to be in? Why?

Why do the pirates of The Black Beast like to meet other pirates?

What is wrong with a ship like Lounge Lizard being in a mess?

Why was Captain Red Beard's plan for Captain Rat so clever?

Next to Captain Red Beard, who has the most important job on The Black Beast? Why?